IELTS WRITING TASK 1 CORRECTIONS

Most Common Mistakes Students Make And How To Avoid Them (Book 1)

JOHNNY CHUONG

Copyright © 2017

All rights reserved.

ISBN: 9781521284421

TEXT COPYRIGHT © [JOHNNY CHUONG]

all rights reserved. No part of this guide may be reproduced in any form without permission in writing from the publisher except in the case of brief quotations embodied in critical articles or reviews.

Legal & disclaimer

The information contained in this book and its contents is not designed to replace or take the place of any form of medical or professional advice; and is not meant to replace the need for independent medical, financial, legal or other professional advice or services, as may be required. The content and information in this book have been provided for educational and entertainment purposes only.

The content and information contained in this book have been compiled from sources deemed reliable, and it is accurate to the best of the author's knowledge, information, and belief. However, the author cannot guarantee its accuracy and validity and cannot be held liable for any errors and/or omissions. Further, changes are periodically made to this book as and when needed. Where appropriate and/or necessary, you must consult a professional (including but not limited to your doctor, attorney, financial advisor or such other professional advisor) before using any of the suggested remedies, techniques, or information in this book.

Upon using the contents and information contained in this book, you agree to hold harmless the author from and against any damages, costs, and expenses, including any legal fees potentially resulting from the application of any of the information provided by this book. This disclaimer applies to any loss, damages or injury caused by the use and application, whether directly or indirectly, of any advice or information presented, whether for breach of contract, tort, negligence, personal injury, criminal intent, or under any other cause of action.

You agree to accept all risks of using the information presented inside this book.

You agree that by continuing to read this book, where appropriate and/or necessary, you shall consult a professional (including but not limited to your doctor, attorney, or financial advisor or such other advisor as needed) before using any of the suggested remedies, techniques, or information in this book.

TABLE OF CONTENT

Introduction
Sample 1
Sample 2
Sample 3
Sample 4
Sample 5
Sample 6
Sample 7
Sample 8
Sample 9
Sample 10
Sample 11
Sample 12
Sample 13
Sample 14
Sample 15
Sample 16
Sample 17
Sample 18
Sample 19
Sample 20
Conclusion
Check Out Other Books

INTRODUCTION

Thank you and congratulate you for downloading the book *"Ielts Writing Task 1 Corrections: Most Common Mistakes Students Make And How To Avoid Them (Book 1)."*

This book reveals numerous common mistakes students make in each type of report of IELTS writing task 1. Then, it will suggest corrections for these all mistakes to help students have a better understanding, avoid unexpected mistakes and achieve a high score in the IELTS Writing task 1.

As the author of this book, I believe that this IETLS writing corrections book will be an indispensable reference and trusted guide for all students who want to maximize their score in IELTS academic writing task 1. I guarantee that all sample essays corrections in this book are practical and not available in any other IELTS textbook or on any website as well. When you read and learn from this book, you will certainly know that it has been written by an experienced teacher, who has spent thousands of hours in a classroom, who understands IELTS students' needs and who is totally able to help them and definitely you are not an exception stay away from the most common mistakes in IELTS writing task 1 and achieve your IELTS writing goal.

Thank you again for purchasing this book, and I hope you enjoy it.

Let's get started!

SAMPLE 1

The graph below compares the number of visits to two now music sites on the web.

Write a report for a university lecturer describing the information shown below.

Source: http://www.ielts-mentor.com/writing-sample/academic-writing-task-1/125-academic-ielts-writing-task-1-sample-37-the-graph-below-compares-the-number-of-visits-to-two-new-music-sites-on-the-web

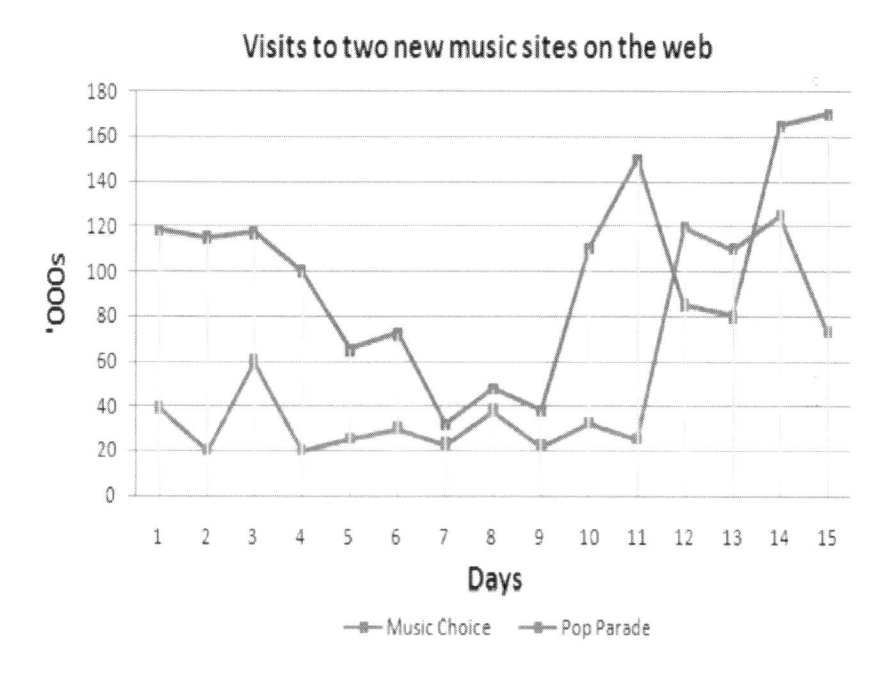

Visits to two new music sites on the web

Original essay:

The line graph provides information in comparison to how many Internet users visiting two new music websites namely Music Choice and Pop Parade on fifteen days.

It is noticeable that the figures for both websites fluctuate violently during this period. However, a much larger number of people visiting Pop Parade compared to Music Choice.

On first day, the amount of users choosing Pop Parade position at precisely 120000 people, is three times higher than that of Music Choice with 40000 users. Later, the figure for Pop Parade experience a considerable and rapid decline to a low of approximately 35000 people on seventh day while the number of Internet users accessing to Music Choice oscillate slightly around 30000 people until day 11.

In the latter half of this period, the amount of visits to Pop Parade soars up suddenly and dramatically to approximately 150000 people on eleventh day before fall abruptly and remains relatively constant until day 13. On the last day, this figure doubles and peaks at around 170000 visits and the gap between two websites in question is widened significantly.

Edited essay:

The line graph provides information ~~in comparison to~~ about ("in comparison to" is used when you compare the items) how many Internet users visiting two new music websites namely Music Choice and Pop Parade on fifteen days.

It is noticeable that the figures for both websites fluctuate violently during this period. However, a much larger number of people visiting Pop Parade compared to Music Choice.

On first day, the amount of users choosing Pop Parade ~~positions~~ stands ("position" is acceptable but it is not really accurate as it means put/arrange) at precisely 120000 people , which is three times higher than that of Music Choice with 40000 users. Later, the figure for Pop Parade experiences a considerable and rapid decline to a low of approximately 35000 people on seventh day while the number of Internet users accessing ~~to~~ ("access" with prepositions when access is used as a noun) Music Choice oscillates slightly around 30000 people until day 11.

In the latter half of this period, the amount of visits to Pop Parade soars up suddenly ~~and dramatically~~ to approximately 150000 people on eleventh day before falling abruptly and remains relatively constant until day 13. On the other hand, after 4 days remaining at less than 40000, the figure of Music Choice recovers to 120000 and stabilizes at 120000. On the last day, ~~this~~

~~figure~~ the number of the former doubles and peaks at around 170000 visits and the gap between two websites in question is widened significantly.

SAMPLE 2

The table below given information about sales of Fairtrade – labelled coffee and bananas in 1999 and 2004 in five European countries.

Source: http://ielts-simon.com/ielts-help-and-english-pr/2015/10/ielts-writing-task-1-table.html

Sales of Fairtrade-labelled coffee and bananas (1999 & 2004)

Coffee	1999 (millions of euros)	2004 (millions of euros)
UK	1.5	20
Switzerland	3	6
Denmark	1.8	2
Belgium	1	1.7
Sweden	0.8	1

Bananas	1999 (millions of euros)	2004 (millions of euros)
UK	15	47
Switzerland	1	5.5
Denmark	0.6	4
Belgium	1.8	1
Sweden	2	0.9

Original essay:

The given tables illustrate data about how much Fairtrade coffee and how many Fairtrade bananas were sold in five different countries in Europe between 1999 and 2004.

Overall, it is clearly seen from the tables that there were much more coffee as well as bananas sold in 2004 than in 1999. Another striking feature is that the UK were the leading country in consuming coffee over 1999-2004 period while the largest number of bananas comsumed was recorded in Switzerland in the same period.

If we look at coffee, the England accounted for the highest amount of coffee consumed with 20 millions of euros; on the contrary, it was Sweden that made up the lowest number of coffee in both years. The other regions including Switzerland, Denmark and Belgium had their figures of bananas in 2004 doubled that in 1999, 3 and 6, 1.8 and 3, and 1 and 1.7 in turn.

Regarding bananas, Switzerland consisted of 15 and 47 millions of euros in 1999 and 2004 respectively, the highest number of bananas recorded. In 1999, only 0.6 millions of euros of bananas sold in Belgium, the lowest number of bananas; however, the smallest number of abovementioned fruit in 2004 belonged to Denmark, 0.9 millions of euros. During 5 years, there was a gradual fall bananas in Sweden, from 1.8 to 1 millions of euros but that in the United Kingdom and Belgium experienced steady improvements by 4,5 and 3,4 millions of euros respectively.

Edited essay:

The given ~~tables illustrate data about how much Fairtrade coffee and how many Fairtrade bananas were sold~~ tables illustrate data on changes in sales of two categories of products, namely fair-trade-labelled coffee and fairtrade-labelled bananas in five different countries in Europe between 1999 and 2004.

Overall, it is clearly seen from the tables that ~~there were much more coffee as well as bananas sold in 2004 than in 1999~~ the amount of money from selling bananas and coffee in 2004 was higher than that in 1999. Another striking feature is that the UK were the leading country in consuming coffee over the period 1999-2004 period while the largest ~~number~~ sales of bananas ~~comsumed~~ was recorded in Switzerland in the same period.

~~If we loook at coffee~~ In terms of coffee, the England ~~accounted for~~ had the highest sales amount of coffee ~~consumed~~ with 20 millions of euros; on the contrary, it was Sweden that ~~made up~~ witnessed the lowest ~~number~~ sales volume of coffee in both years surveyed. The other regions including

Switzerland, Denmark and Belgium had their figures of bananas in 2004 doubled that in 1999, 3 and 6, 1.8 and 3, and 1 and 1.7 ~~in turn~~ respectively.

Regarding bananas, the sales of Switzerland ~~consisted of~~ were 15 and 47 millions of euros in 1999 and 2004 respectively, which were the highest numbers of bananas recorded. In 1999, only 0.6 ~~millions of euros~~ million Euros of bananas were sold in Belgium, the lowest ~~number~~ figure of bananas. However, the ~~smallest number~~ lowest sales of the abovementioned fruit in 2004 belonged to Denmark, 0.9 ~~millions of euros~~ million Euros. During 5 years, there was a gradual fall in the sale volume of bananas in Sweden, from 1.8 to 1 ~~million of euros~~ million Euros but that in the United Kingdom and Belgium experienced steady improvements by 4.5 and 3.4 ~~millions of euros~~ million Euros respectively.

Sample essay:

http://www.ielts-mentor.com/writing-sample/academic-writing-task-1/2356-academic-ielts-writing-task-1-sample-174-sales-of-fairtrade-labelled-coffee-and-bananas

SAMPLE 3

The tables below give information about sales of Fairtrade-labelled coffee and bananas in 1999 and 2004 in five European countries.*

Summarise the information by selecting and reporting the main features, and make comparisons where relevant.

Write at least 150 words.

Sales of Fairtrade-labelled coffee and bananas (1999 & 2004)

Coffee	1999 (millions of euros)	2004 (millions of euros)
UK	1.5	20
Switzerland	3	6
Denmark	1.8	2
Belgium	1	1.7
Sweden	0.8	1

Bananas	1999 (millions of euros)	2004 (millions of euros)
Switzerland	15	47
UK	1	5.5
Belgium	0.6	4
Sweden	1.8	1
Denmark	2	0.9

Source: http://ielts-simon.com/ielts-help-and-english-pr/2015/10/ielts-writing-task-1-table.html

Original essay:

The tables compare the amount of money in millions of euros that the Fairtrade- labelled coffee and bananas were sole in 5 countries in Europe between the year 1999 and 2004.

Overall, UK and Switzerland consumed these products most among 5 countries in the given years.

UK saw a dramatic growth in the sale of bananas from 1 in 1999 to 5.5 in 2004 and a much more significant increase in the sale of coffee from 1.5 to 20. In Swetzerland market, there was a double in the sale of coffee and more than a triple in that of bananas to reach 6 and 47 in 2004 respectively.

In contrast, in Denmark and Sweden, there was a slight increase by 0.2 in the sales of coffee to obtain 2 and 1 in 2004 respectively. Even the sales of bananas of these 2 countries decreased about a half, from 2 to 0.9 for the former and from 1.8 to1for the latter. In Belgium, the sale of coffee grew by 0.7 to 1.7 in 2004 however bananas brought 3.4 more in 2004 compared to 1999 to reach 4.

Edited essay:

The tables compare the amount of ~~money~~ sales in millions of euros that the Fairtrade- labelled coffee and bananas ~~were sole~~ in 5 countries in Europe between the year 1999 and 2004.

Overall, UK and Switzerland consumed ~~these products most~~ the largest quantities of these products among 5 countries in the given years.

UK saw ~~a~~ dramatic growth ("growth" is an uncountable noun) in the sales of bananas from 1 in 1999 to 5.5 in 2004 and a much more significant increase in the sales of coffee from 1.5 to 20. In ~~Swetzerland~~ Swiss market, there was ~~a~~ double ("double" is an uncountable noun with this meaning) in the sales of coffee and more than a triple in ~~that~~ those of bananas to reach 6 and 47 in 2004 respectively.

In contrast, in Denmark and Sweden, there was a slight increase by 0.2 in the sales of coffee to ~~obtain~~ reach selling revenues of 2 and 1 in 2004 respectively. Even the sales of bananas of these 2 countries decreased about a half, from 2 to 0.9 for the former and from 1.8 to1for the latter. In Belgium, the sales of coffee grew by 0.7 to 1.7 in 2004 however bananas brought 3.4 more in 2004 compared to 1999 to reach 4.

SAMPLE 4

The graph below shows the proportion of the population aged 65 and over between 1940 and 2040 in three different countries.

Summarise the information by selecting and reporting the main features, and make comparisons where relevant.

Source: http://www.ielts-mentor.com/writing-sample/academic-writing-task-1/1030-academic-ielts-writing-task-1-sample-93-proportion-of-the-population-aged-65-and-over-between-1940-and-2040

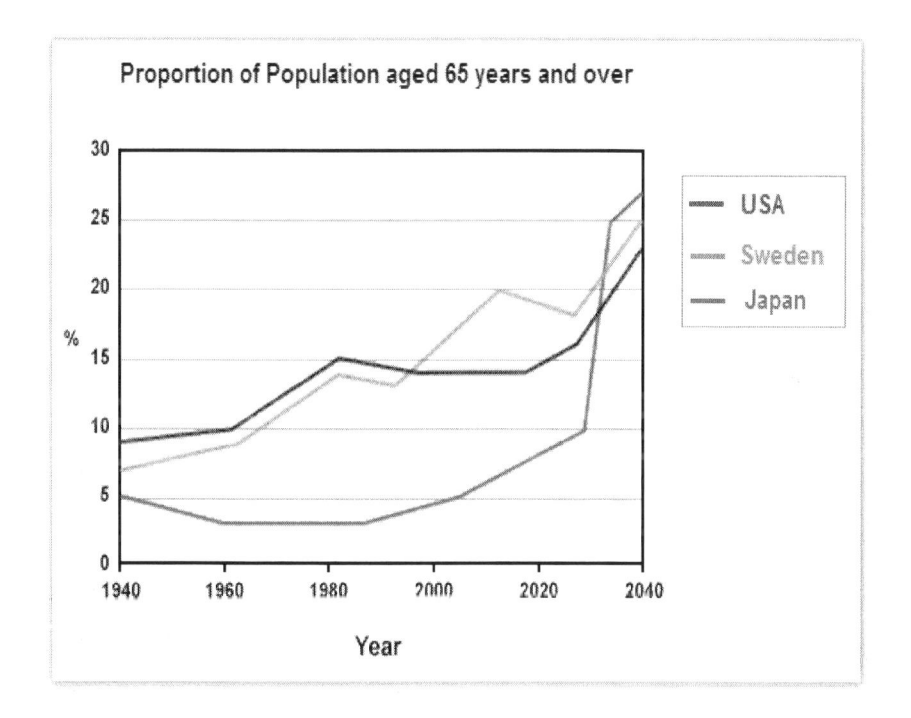

Original essay:

A glance at the line graph provide the figures of the people aged 65 upwards during a century in Japan, Sweden and USA

Thoughtout the century, the number of elderly people in three different countries increase. The rate this in Japan is lowest in 1940 and highest in

2040

From 1940 to 2030, it is fluctuated to 5 percent to 10 percent in Japan and to under 10 percent to almost 18 percent in Sweden and the USA.

In spite of some fluctuation in the expected percentages, the proportion of this countries estimated to grow. There are dramatic increase between 2030 and 2040 in the Japan and it is higher than swenden and USA at about 28 percent, by which time. The figures of swenden is increase to 25 percent, compared with increase to about 18 percent of rate in USA.

Edited essay:

A glance at the line graph provides the ~~figures of~~ figure for the people aged 65 and over ~~upwards~~ during a century in Japan, Sweden and USA

~~Thoughtout~~ Throughout the century, the number of elderly people in three different countries is expected to increase. ~~The rate this~~ The population rate in Japan ~~is~~ was the lowest in 1940 and is predicted to be the highest in 2040.

From 1940 to 2030, it is fluctuated to 5 percent to 10 percent in Japan and to under 10 percent to almost 18 percent in Sweden and the USA.

In spite of some fluctuation in the expected percentages, the proportion of ~~this countries~~ people in these countries is estimated to grow. There ~~are~~ is a dramatic increase between 2030 and 2040 in the Japan and it is higher than ~~swenden~~ Sweden and USA at about 28 percent, by which time. The figures ~~of~~ for ~~swenden~~ Sweden ~~is~~ will increase to 25 percent, compared with an increase ~~to~~ of about 18 percent ~~of rate~~ in USA.

SAMPLE 5

The bar chart below shows the percentage of unemployed graduates, aged 20-24 in one European country over a two-year period.

Summarise the information by selecting and reporting the main features, and making comparisons where relevant.

Source: http://ieltsmaterial.com/ielts-writing-practice-test-13-from-ielts-practice-test-plus-03/

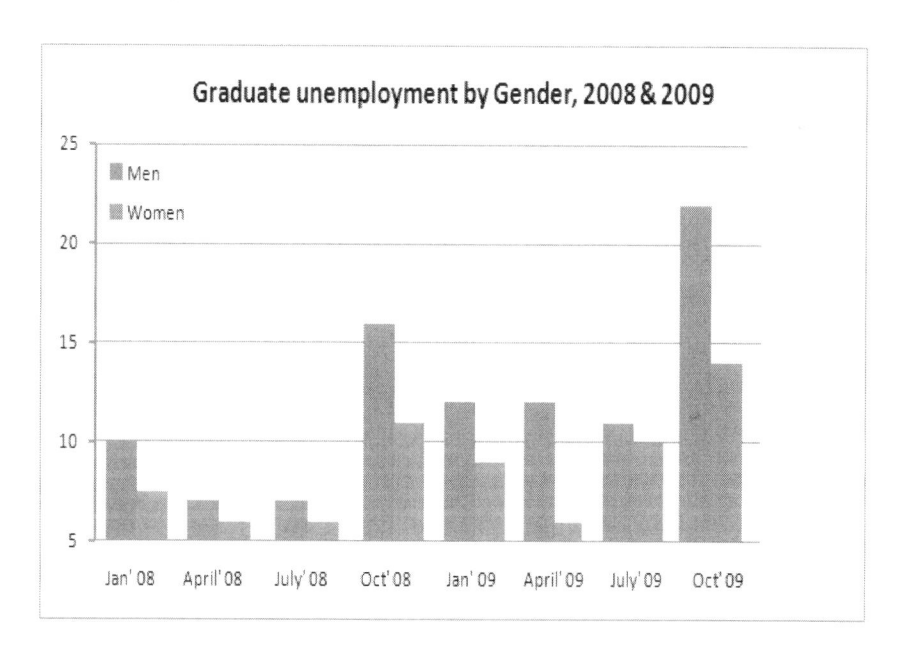

Graduate unemployment by Gender, 2008 & 2009

Original essay:

The bar chart illustrates the proportions of people aged 20-24 who graduated bur could not find suitable jobs in an European country over the course of two years 2008 and 2009. Overall, the participation rates were always higher with the men in the whole period. It can be seen that these proportions at the end of each year accounted larger than these in the beginning.

In 2008, the groups of 20-24 year old unemployed graduates accounted for

10 and 8% in January for men and women respectively. These figures witnessed declines in following months to 8 and 6% for men and women in April. There were significant increases with both genders in October, reaching 16% by men and 11% by women.

In the subsequent year, both genders started with higher points, compared the 2008, at 12% for males and 9% for females. This proportions remained unchanged for the males, while reduced to below 5% for the females in April. The females then picked up sharply in stages, hitting its peak at 15% in October. In the meantime, the males' figure, after a slight decrease in July, rocketed to its highest point at 22% in October 2009.

Edited essay:

The bar chart illustrates the proportions of ~~people aged 20-24~~ 20-to-24-year-olds who graduated but could not find suitable jobs in terms of gender in a European country ~~over the course of two years 2008 and 2009~~ between 2008 and 2009. Overall, ~~the participation rates were always higher with the men in the whole period~~ The rate of male unemployment was always higher than that of female unemployment in the whole period surveyed. ~~It can be seen that these proportions at the end of each year accounted larger than these in the beginning~~ It can be seen that there was a gradual increase in the proportion of unemployed graduates in every period of the whole.

In 2008, the groups of 20-24 year old unemployed graduates in January ~~accounted for~~ made up 10 and 8% of the total ~~in~~ January for men and women respectively. These figures witnessed declines in following months to 8 and 6% for men and women in April. By contrast, there were significant increases ~~with~~ in the figure for both genders in October, reaching 16% by men and 11% by women.

In the subsequent year, both genders started with higher points, compared with the figures in the 2008, at 12% for males and 9% for females. ~~This proportions~~ The proportion remained unchanged for the males, while it reduced to below 5% for the females in April. ~~The females then picked up sharply in stages, hitting its peak at 15% in October~~ Especially, the percentage of unemployed female graduates increased sharply before reaching a peak of 15% in October. ~~In the meantime~~ Meanwhile, the males' figure, after a slight decrease in July, rocketed to its highest point at 22% in

October 2009.

Sample essay:

http://www.ielts-mentor.com/writing-sample/academic-writing-task-1/1943-academic-ielts-writing-task-1-sample-152-the-percentage-of-unemployed-graduates

SAMPLE 6

The bar chart below shows the results of a survey conducted by a personnel department at a major company. The survey was carried out on two groups of workers: those aged from 18-30 and those aged 45-60, and shows factors affecting their work performance.

Write a report for a university lecturer describing the information shown below.

You should write at least 150 words.

Source: http://www.ielts-exam.net/academic_writing_samples_task_1/473/

Factors affecting work performance

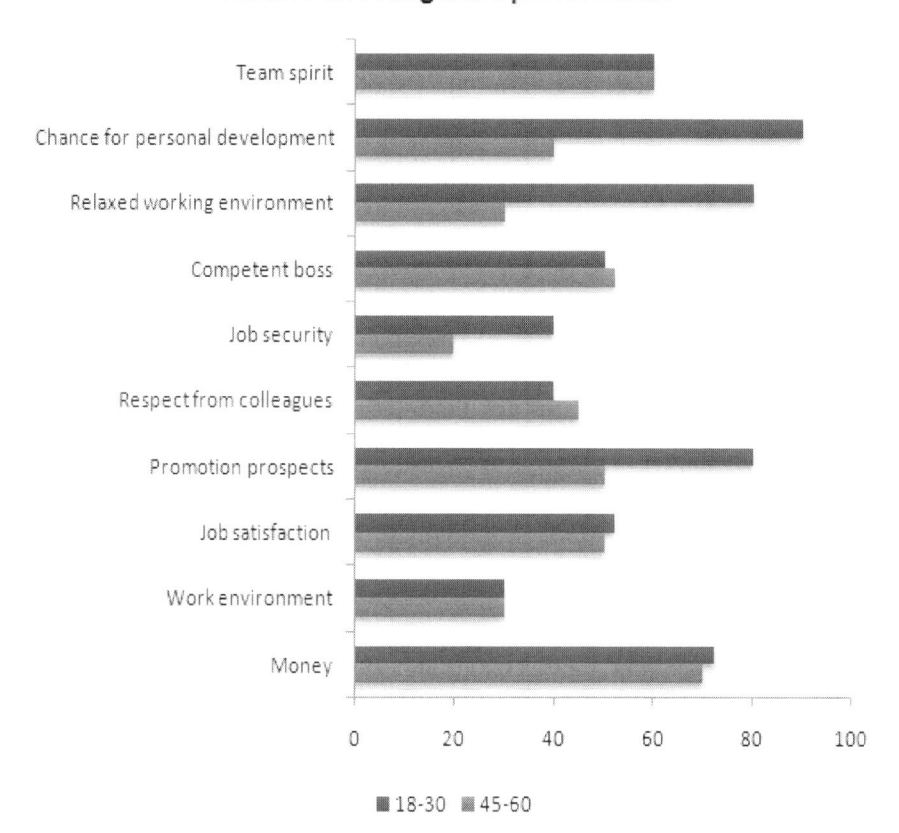

[Bar chart showing factors affecting work performance for two age groups (18-30 and 45-60), with approximate values:
- Team spirit: 60, 60
- Chance for personal development: 90, 40
- Relaxed working environment: 80, 30
- Competent boss: 50, 52
- Job security: 40, 20
- Respect from colleagues: 40, 45
- Promotion prospects: 80, 50
- Job satisfaction: 52, 50
- Work environment: 30, 30
- Money: 72, 70]

Original essay:

The bar chart illustrates the result of a survey on two different age groups on the factors influencing the employees on how they do their tasks.

Overall, it is clear that there are two kinds of factors shown in this chart, which are the internal and external one. The internal factors include team spirit, competent boss, respect from colleagues and job satisfaction while the external factors are the other ones.

Beginning with the internal factors, above 50% of both age groups are effected by these elements. The team spirit is showed to have the strongest effect in this type of factor, with the numbers in both groups are 60%.

Moving to the next type of factors, the external one seems to affect the younger people more than the older one. The proportions for chance for development and relaxed working environment, job security, promotion prospects for the younger age almost doubled that for the older one. It is also interesting to note that the younger people care most about their chances for development and promotion with the number for these two factors are about 90% and 80% respectively while the older people one is affected the most by money with the number of 70% indicators for this one.

Edited essay:

The bar chart illustrates the result of a survey on two different age groups on the factors influencing the employees on how they do their tasks.

Overall, ~~it is clear that there are two kinds of factors shown in this chart, which are the internal and external one. The internal factors include team spirit, competent boss, respect from colleagues and job satisfaction while the external factors are the other ones.~~ (The overview needs you to give the overall trend, not grouping the factors. Moreover, it is very difficult to group the factors as one can be both internal and external).

Suggestion: Overall, similarities between two age groups can be seen in the majority of factors, except for chance for development, working environment and promotion prospects which see a significant higher percentage of those from 18 to 30.

~~Beginning with~~ Concerning the internal factors, above 50% of both age groups are ~~effected~~ affected by these elements. ~~The~~ Team spirit ~~is showed to have~~ has the strongest effect ~~in this type of factor~~ compared with other factors in the same category, ~~with the numbers in both groups are 60%~~ with 60% for each group. Meanwhile, the remaining elements have almost the same percentage at around 50%.

Moving to the next type of factors, the external one seems to affect ~~the~~ younger people more than the older one. The proportions for chance for development and relaxed working environment, job security, promotion prospects for the younger age almost ~~doubled~~ that for the older one. It is also interesting to note that the younger people care most about their chances for development and promotion with ~~the number for these two factors are about~~ 90% and 80% respectively while the older people one is affected the most by money with ~~the number of~~ 70% ~~indicators for this one~~.

Sample essay:

http://www.ielts-exam.net/academic_writing_samples_task_1/473/

SAMPLE 7

The bar chart below gives information about the number of students studying Computer Science at a UK university between 2010 and 2012.

Summarise the information by selecting and reporting the main features, and make comparisons where relevant.

Source: http://www.ielts-exam.net/academic_writing_samples_task_1/718/

Home and International students, 2010-2012

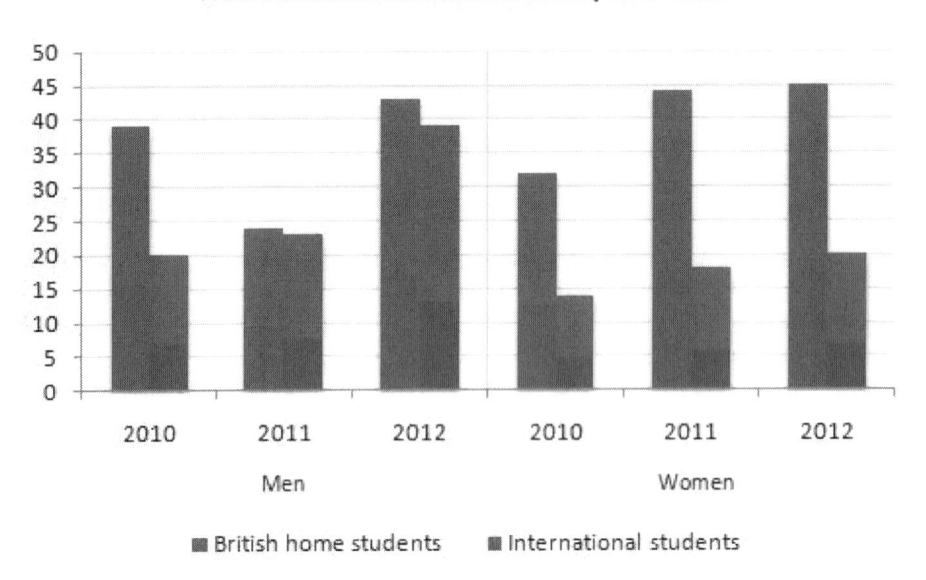

Original essay:

The bar chart illustrates the number of male and female students who keen on learning Computer Science at a UK university from 2010 to 2012.

Overall, the local students in Britain account for the highest number. In addition, the number of foreign students increased significantly in both side: men and women.

As s shown in the graph, in 2010 the figure for male students in Britain was by far more than that of male international students (39 students and 20 students). However, the number of male home students fluctuated during the period with 42 student in 2012 after dipping dramatically in 2011. By contrast, the number of male international students increased stably until 2012 with 38 students.

As the same period, the number of female students in Britain was higher than that of female international students (32 students and 13 student), .This figure kept growing up considerably in both Home and International students. In 2012, it was known that 45 female home students and 20 female international students studied Computer Science.

Edited essay:

The bar chart illustrates the number of male and female students who were keen on learning Computer Science at a UK university from 2010 to 2012.

Overall, the local students in Britain accounted for the highest number. In addition, the number of foreign students increased significantly in both side: men and women.

Suggestion: Overall, more local students majored in Computer Science than international ones over the course of three years. In addition, there was an increasing trend in the number of foreign students in both genders between 2010 and 2012.

As s shown in the graph, in 2010 the figure for male students in Britain was by far more than that of male international students (39 students and 20 students). However, the number of male home students fluctuated during the period with 42 student in 2012 after dipping dramatically in 2011. By contrast, the number of male international students increased stably until 2012 with 38 students.

As In the same period, the number of female students in Britain was higher than that of female international students (32 students and 13 student), .This figure The figures for both home and overseas students kept growing up considerably steadily in both Home and International students. In 2012, it was known that 45 female home students and 20 female international students ~~studied~~ studying/who studied Computer Science.

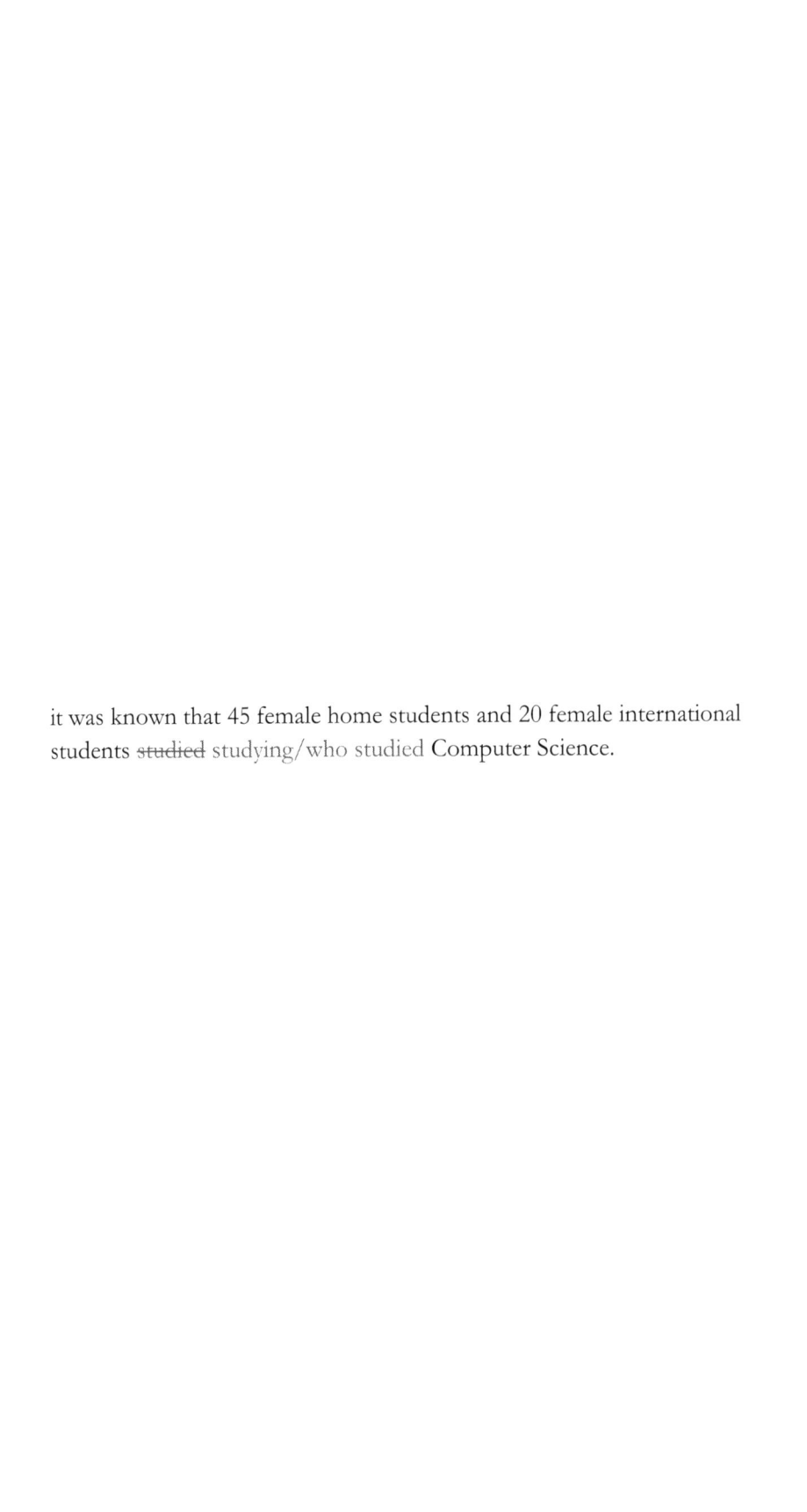

SAMPLE 8

The essay below is 151 words long. I've tried to make it as simple as possible, but it's still good enough to get a band 9.

Source: http://ielts-simon.com/ielts-help-and-english-pr/2010/08/ielts-writing-task-1-full-essay.html

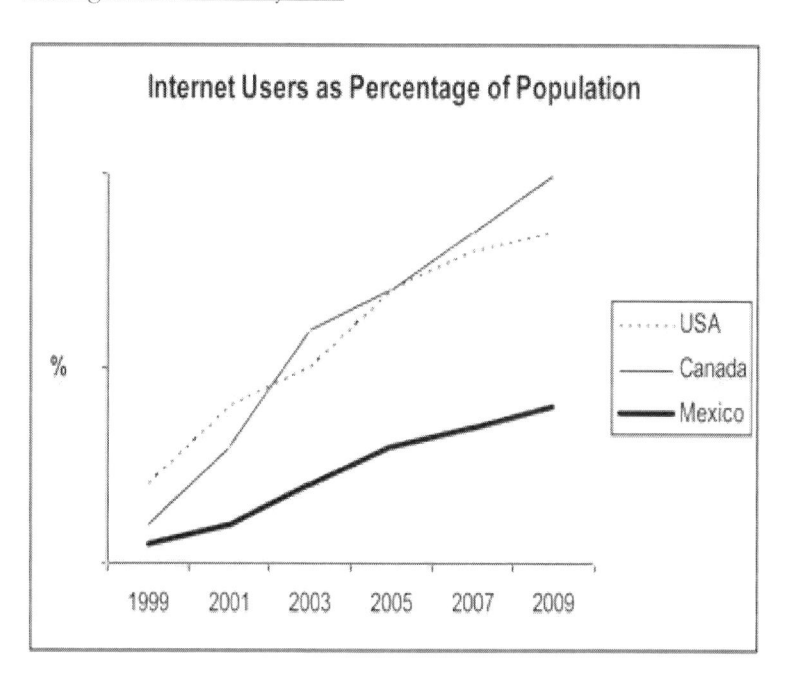

Original essay:

The chart shows information on the percentage of internet users in USA, Canada, Mexico from 1999 to 2009.

Overall, internet users rate rose quickly in USA and Canada, in Mexico it increased gradually from 1999 to 2009.

From 1999 to 2001, internet users rate in USA was higher than in Canada and Mexico. In 2002, there was equal to the ratio of internet users in two countries which were USA and Canada. Mexico's percentage of internet users rose steadily and was shortest than two that countries from 1999 to 2002.

After 2002, the rate of internet users in USA, Canada and Mexico had a rising significantly trend. In 2005, USA and Canada had the percentage of internet users which were equal. From 2002 to 2009 the percentage of internet users in Canada was higher than USA, and it had a tallest in three this countries in 2009.

Edited essay:

The chart shows information on the percentage of internet users in USA, Canada, and Mexico from 1999 to 2009.

Overall, internet users rate rose quickly in USA and Canada, while in Mexico, it increased gradually from 1999 to 2009.

From 1999 to 2001, ~~internet users rate~~ the proportion of internet users (avoid repetition) in USA was higher than in Canada and Mexico. In 2002, ~~there was equal to~~ (this noun is inappropriate for the context and task 1) the ratio of internet users in two countries which were USA and Canada. ~~Mexico's percentage~~ In comparison/ In contrast of internet users rose steadily and was shortest than ~~two that countries~~ the figures for USA and Canada from 1999 to 2002.

~~After 2002,~~ From 2002 onwards, the rate of internet users in USA, Canada and Mexico ~~had a rising significantly trend~~ experienced an upward trend. In 2005, USA and Canada had the percentage of internet users which were equal. From 2002 to 2009 the percentage of internet users in Canada was higher than that in USA, and it ~~had a tallest in three this countries~~ ranked first in 2009.

SAMPLE 9

The charts below show the number of Japanese tourists travelling abroad between 1985 and 1995 and Australias share of the Japanese tourist market.

Write a report for a university lecturer describing the information shown below.

You should write at least 150 words.

Source: http://www.ielts-exam.net/academic_writing_samples_task_1/130/

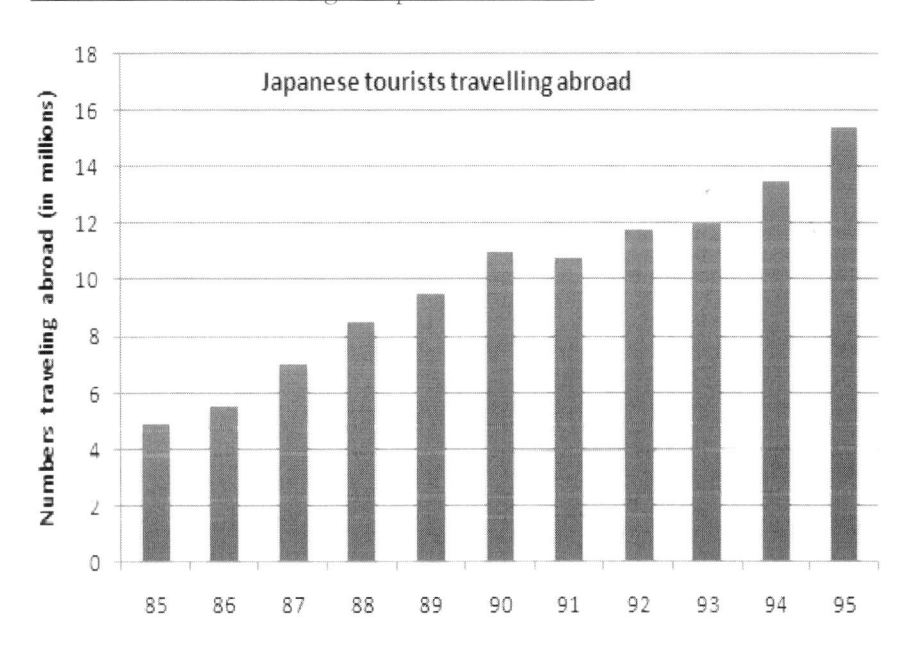

Australia's share of Japan's tourist market

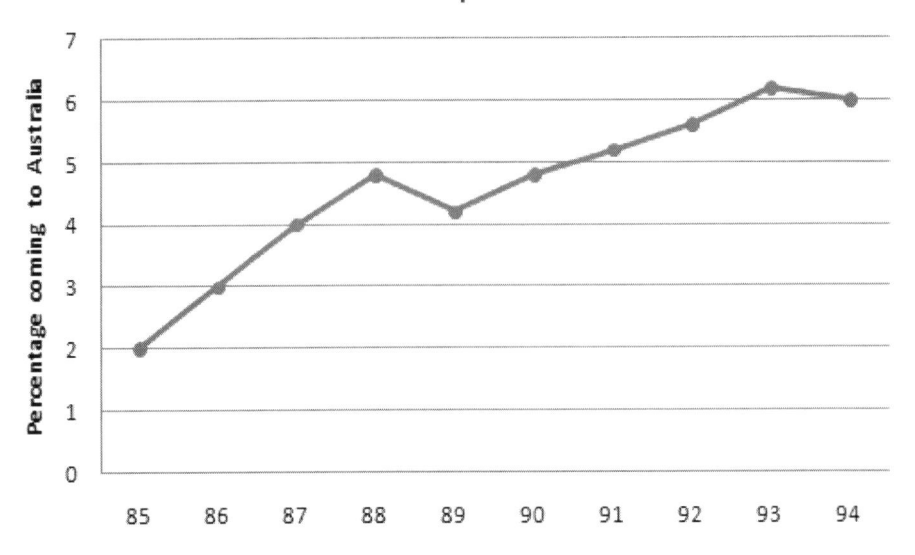

Y-axis: Percentage coming to Australia (0-7)
X-axis: 85, 86, 87, 88, 89, 90, 91, 92, 93, 94

Original essay:

The data about travelling in foreign countries of Japanese from 1985 to 1995 was shown in two charts. The bar graph shows the number of Japanese tourists going abroad and the line graph shows the percantage Japanese selecting Australia to travel.

Overall, the travel trend to other countries of Japanese icreases steadly except a little decrease in 1991. Similarly, exception for 1990 and 1995, there is a rising trend of Japanese to Australia from 1985 to 1995.

In 1985, 5 million people in Japan traveled to other countries and 2% of them went to Australia. The number contiuned to grow constantly up to 1990 with 11 million people and decline slightly in 1991 with 10.5 million ones. The percentage visiting Australia rose significantly up to 1989 with 5% but it dropped to 4.3% in 1990.

From 1992 to 1995, there was a steady growth in number of Japanese tourist travelling abroad. For the rate of visiting Australia in Japan, after recovering in 1991 with 5%, the rising trend lasted to 1994 with 6.2%. In 1995, the rate was decreased slightly by 6%.

Edited essay:

The data about travelling in foreign countries of Japanese from 1985 to 1995 was shown in two charts. The bar graph shows the number of Japanese tourists going abroad and the line graph ~~shows~~ illustrates the percentage Japanese selecting Australia to travel.

Overall, the ~~travel trend~~ travelling to other countries of Japanese tended to increase ~~icreases~~ steadily except a little decrease in 1991. Similarly, ~~exception for 1990 and 1995~~ with the exception of figures in 1990 and 1995, there is a rising trend ~~of~~ in the number of Japanese to Australia from 1985 to 1995.

In 1985, 5 million people in Japan travelled to other countries and 2% of them went to Australia. The number ~~contiuned~~ continued ~~to grow~~ growing constantly ~~up to~~ until 1990 with 11 million people and decline slightly in 1991 with 10.5 million ones. The percentage ~~visiting~~ visitors to Australia rose significantly ~~up to~~ until 1989 with 5% ~~but it droped~~ before dropping to 4.3% in 1990.

From 1992 to 1995, there was a steady growth in number of Japanese tourist travelling abroad. For the rate of visiting Australia in Japan, after recovering in 1991 with 5%, the rising trend lasted to 1994 with 6.2%. In 1995, ~~the rate was~~ this figure decreased slightly by 6%.

SAMPLE 10

The graph below shows the number of books read by men and women at Burnaby Public Library from 2011 to 2014.

Summarise the information by selecting and reporting the main features, and make comparisons where relevant.

Source: http://www.ielts-exam.net/academic_writing_samples_task_1/854/

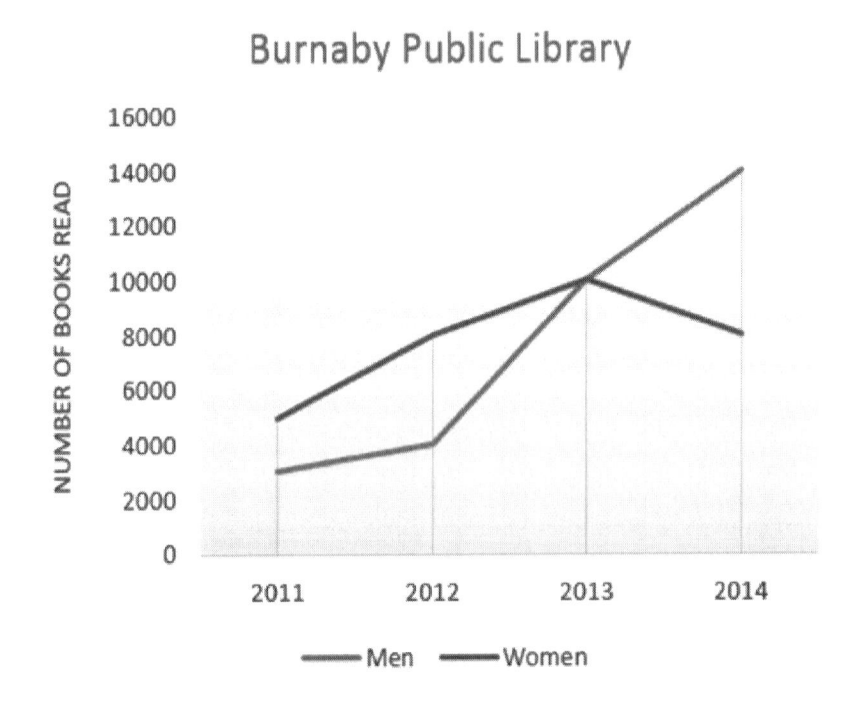

Burnaby Public Library

[Line graph showing NUMBER OF BOOKS READ (0 to 16000) on y-axis and years 2011-2014 on x-axis, with lines for Men and Women]

Original essay:

The line graph gives the information about Burnaby Public Library in term of numbers of books that men and women read between 2011 and 2014.

Overall, there were significantly different trends between man and woman readers. While number of man readers increased considerably from 2011 to

2014, this number of woman experienced a fall at the same period.

In 2011, number of men read books in the library was approximately 3000, which was lower than number of woman readers (about 5000). From 2012 to 2013, there was a sharp rise in number of men read book while women's number incresed gradually and reached a maximum number of reader at about 10000.

In 2013- 2014 period, number of man readers continued growing and peaked at nearly 14000. Otherwise, this of woman fell to about 8000 in 2014.

Edited essay:

The line graph gives the information about Burnaby Public Library in term of ~~numbers of books that~~ how many books men and women read between 2011 and 2014.

Overall, there were significantly different trends between man and woman readers. While number of man readers increased considerably from 2011 to 2014, this number of woman experienced a fall at the same period.

In 2011, number of men read books in the library was approximately 3000, which was lower than ~~number~~ that of woman readers (about 5000). From 2012 to 2013, there was a sharp rise in number of men read book while women's number increased gradually and reached a ~~maximum number of reader~~ peak/ reach a peak at about 10000.

In 2013- 2014 ~~period~~, ~~number~~ the quantity (avoid repetition) of man readers continued growing and peaked at nearly 14000. Otherwise, ~~this of woman fell to about 8000 in 2014~~ the figure of woman saw a slight decrease by almost 2000 and in 2014, only 8000 women read books at this library.

SAMPLE 11

The chart below shows the percentage of male and female teachers in six different types of educational setting in the UK in 2010.

Source: http://www.ielts-exam.net/academic_writing_samples_task_1/726/

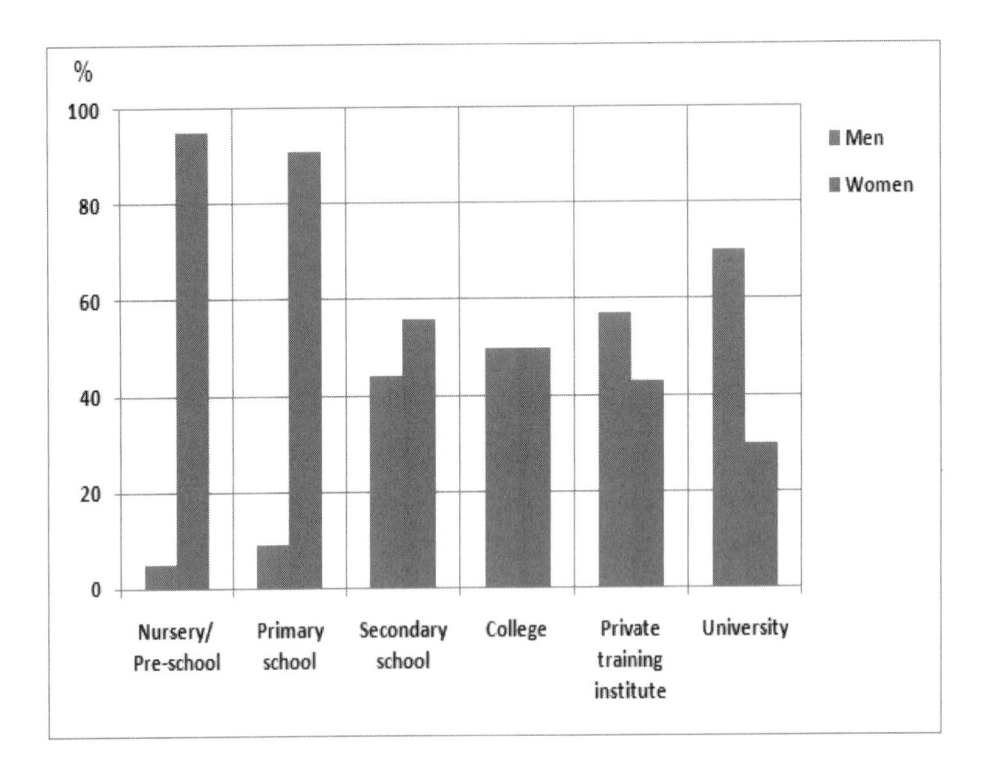

Original essay:

The bar chart indicates data on gender of teachers in six different kinds of educational institution in United Kingdom in 2010.

Overall, the number of women choosing teaching work in UK is more than men. While female teachers tend to teach in pre-school or primary school, male teachers enjoy working in higher education.

The percentage of women teaching in nursery and primary school are fractionally more than men. About 97% teachers in nursery school are women and just 3% teachers are men. This figure is quite similar to primary school, with around 90% female teachers and nearly 5% male teachers

In three types of educational setting: secondary school, college and private training institute, the proportion of male and female teachers is almost equally. In particularly, the number teacher working in college in both genders is the same, at precisely 40%. By contrast, in university, male professor rates increase dramatically to approximately 70%, and male professors account for less than 40%.

Edited essay:

The bar chart indicates ~~data~~ proportion on gender of teachers in six different kinds of educational institutions in the United Kingdom in 2010.

Overall, the number of women choosing teaching work in UK ~~is~~ was more than men in 2010. While female teachers tended to teach in pre-school or primary school, male teachers enjoyed working in higher education.

The percentage of women teaching in nursery and primary school ~~are~~ was ~~fractionally~~ considerably more than men. About 97% teachers in nursery school ~~are~~ were women ~~and~~, while just 3% teachers ~~are~~ were men. This figure ~~is~~ was quite similar to that of primary school, with around 90% female teachers and nearly 5% male teachers

In three other types of educational setting: secondary school, college and private training institute, the proportions of male and female teachers ~~is~~ were almost equally. In particularly, the number teacher working in college in both genders ~~is~~ was the same, at precisely 40%. By contrast, in university, male professor rates increased dramatically to approximately 70%, ~~and~~ whereas ~~male~~ female professors accounted for less than 40%.

SAMPLE 12

The maps below show the village of Stokeford in 1930 and in 2010.

Summarise the information by selecting and reporting the main features, and make comparisons where relevant.

Source: http://www.ielts-mentor.com/writing-sample/academic-writing-task-1/1920-academic-ielts-writing-task-1-sample-145-village-of-stokeford-in-1930-and-2010

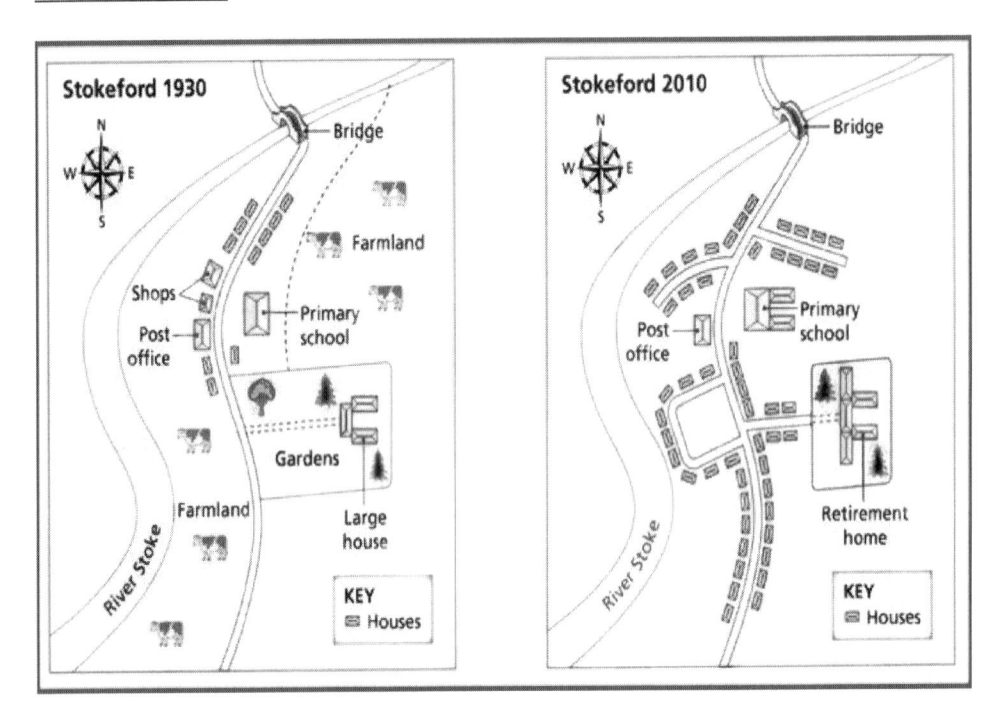

Original essay:

The two maps illustrate changes that happened in Stokeford during an 80-year period, from 1930 to 2010.

Overall, it can clearly be seen that all of the original farmlands have been gone, mostly to give ways for newly built houses. In 2010, a retirement home and a number of roads were also constructed in the village of Stokeford.

According to the maps, Stokeford was largely occupied by farmlands in 1930. The first farm area bordered on River Stoke whereas the second one located at the North East End of the village. However, in 2010, both farmland areas were replaced by a housing complex along the main road. While the post office remained the same throughout 80 years, the shopping zone became residential housing estate as well. Four secondary roads were therefore constructed accordingly to convenniently connect the houses with the village's main road.

Although the primary school was sited at the same location, it was noticeably expanded in 2010. The gardens which once was seen opposite to the first farmland had been divided into two different sections: one for residential purposes and the other half became a retirement home with trees and shelters.

Stokeford's major transportation facilities, which are the a main road and a bridge across River Stoke kept unchanged despi9te all of the transformation witnessed over the period of 80 years.

Edited essay:

The two maps illustrate changes that happened in Stokeford during an 80-year period, from 1930 to 2010.

Overall, it can clearly be seen that all of the original farmlands have been gone, mostly to give ways ~~for~~ to (we could use "reconstructed"/"were changed into" or "make way for") newly built houses. In 2010, a retirement home and a number of roads were also constructed in the village of Stokeford.

According to the maps, Stokeford was largely occupied by farmlands in 1930. ~~The first farm area bordered on River Stoke~~ River Stoke was bordered by the first farm area (usually, we use "border" in passive voice) whereas the second one was located ~~at~~ in the North East End of the village. However, in 2010, both farmland areas were replaced ~~by~~ with a housing complex along the main road. While the post office remained the same throughout 80 years, the shopping zone became residential housing estate as well. Four secondary roads were therefore constructed ~~accordingly to convenniently connect~~ conveniently to connect the houses with the village's main road.

Although the primary school was sited at the same location, it was noticeably expanded in 2010. The gardens which once ~~was~~ were seen opposite to the first farmland ~~had been~~ were divided into two different sections: one for residential purposes and the other half became a retirement home with trees and shelters.

Stokeford's major transportation facilities, which ~~are the~~ includes a main road and a bridge across River Stoke kept unchanged despi9te all of the transformation was witnessed over the period of 80 years.

SAMPLE 13

The pie charts below show the average household expenditures in a country in 1950 and 2010.

Summarise the information by selecting and reporting the main features, and make comparisons where relevant.

Source: http://www.ielts-exam.net/academic_writing_samples_task_1/706/

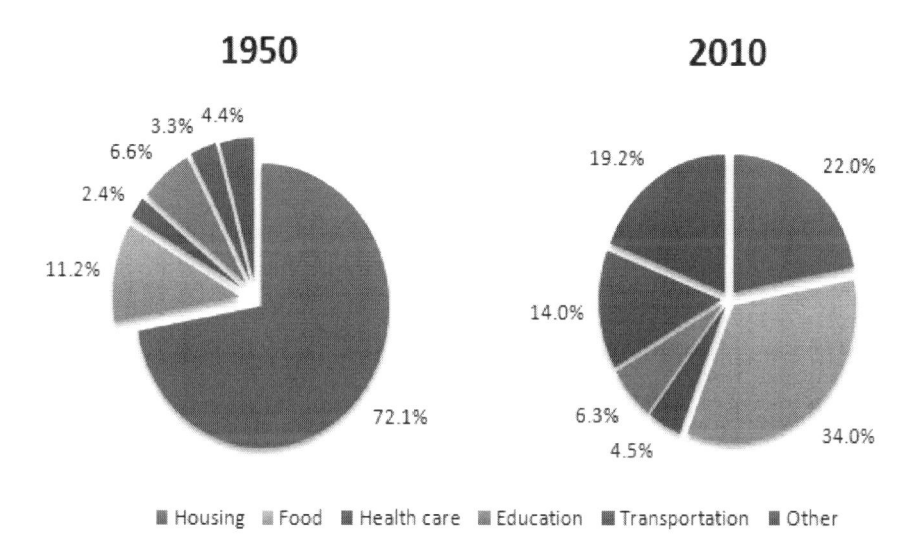

1950

- 72.1%
- 11.2%
- 2.4%
- 6.6%
- 3.3%
- 4.4%

2010

- 22.0%
- 34.0%
- 4.5%
- 6.3%
- 14.0%
- 19.2%

■ Housing ■ Food ■ Health care ■ Education ■ Transportation ■ Other

Original essay:

Two pie charts show data about the household expenditure of two average US families in 1970 and 2004. Those household includes food, transport, entertainment, mortgage, clothing and childcare.

At a first glance, mortgage and childcare have a significant growth while entertainment remains steadily and others decrease over three decades.

In 1970, mortgage got 26% of household expenditure and rose to nearly two times in 2004. Similarly, with only 1% in 1970, childcare jumped to 10% after 34 years. Entertainment is the only household that does not have any fluctuation in a long period of time with 13%.

In contrast, food, transport and clothing have a decrease percentage between 1970 and 2004. Accounting for a quarter of household expenditure in 1970, food expenditure fell marketly in 2004 by 12%. Payments for transport and clothing have the same tendency. 13% of transport and 22% of clothing expenditure were recorded in 1970, but in 2004 those reduced to 5% and 10% respectively according to the pie charts.

Edited essay:

The two pie charts show data about the household expenditure of two average US families in 1970 and 2004. ~~Those household includes food, transport, entertainment, mortgage, clothing and childcare~~.

At a first glance, mortgage and childcare have a significant growth while entertainment remains steadily and others decrease over three decades. Although food accounted for the largest proportion in total expenditure in 1970, mortgage became the category that was spent the most in the latter year.

In 1970, mortgage got 26% of household expenditure and rose to nearly two times in 2004. Similarly, with only 1% in 1970, childcare jumped to 10% after 34 years. Entertainment ~~is~~ was the only household that ~~does~~ did not have any fluctuation in a long period of time with 13%.

In contrast, food, transport and clothing ~~have~~ experienced a decrease in percentage between 1970 and 2004. Accounting for a quarter of household expenditure in 1970, food expenditure fell ~~marketly~~ considerably in 2004 ~~by~~ to 12%. Payments for transport and clothing ~~have~~ saw the same tendency. 13% of transport and 22% of clothing expenditure were recorded in 1970, but in 2004 those reduced to 5% and 10% respectively according to the pie charts.

SAMPLE 14

The charts below show the results of a questionnaire that asked visitors to the Parkway Hotel how they rated the hotel's customer service. The same questionnaire was given to 100 guests in the years 2005 and 2010.

Source: http://ielts-simon.com/ielts-help-and-english-pr/2016/07/ielts-writing-task-1-customer-service-pie-charts-1.html

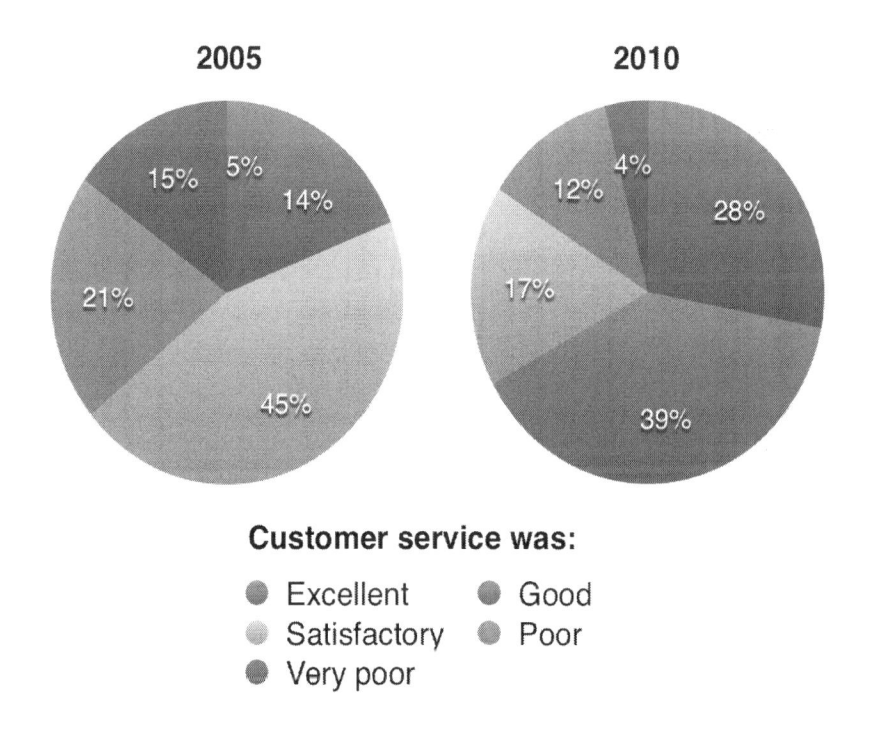

2005
- 15%
- 5%
- 14%
- 21%
- 45%

2010
- 12%
- 4%
- 28%
- 17%
- 39%

Customer service was:
- Excellent
- Good
- Satisfactory
- Poor
- Very poor

Original essay:

The pie charts compare the opinion rates of visitors in term of customer sevice at the Parkway Hotel in 5 years , 2005 and 2010

Overall, the percentages of customer sevice rated for each of 5 answers changed significantly from 2005 to 2010. While the answer excellent and good increased, the figure for the other 3 comment about hotel's service decreased sharply.

In 2005, the proportion of guests felt excellent were 5%, but this rose by to 28 % in 2010. Likewise, 14% of visitors described good in 2015 and 39 % in 2010 - was the highest.

In contrast, the percentages of people who had negative coments about hotel fell. The most dramatic fall was in the answer satisfactory by 28%. There was a decline in the figure for the opinion that poor. In addition, the Parkway Hotel saw a dramatic decrease in the rates of visitors felt very poor, which was the lowest – 4% in 2010.

Edited essay:

The pie charts compare the opinion rates of visitors in term of customer service at the Parkway Hotel in 5 years two different years, 2005 and 2010

Overall, the percentages of customer service rated for each of 5 answers for five levels of satisfaction changed significantly from 2005 to 2010. While the answer for excellent and good increased, the figure for the other 3 comments about hotel's service decreased sharply.

In 2005, the proportion of guests felt excellent were 5%, but this rose by significantly to 28 % in 2010. Likewise, 14% of visitors described the service as good in 2015 and this figure increased to 39 % in 2010 was the highest , which constituted for the most in customer's rate.

In contrast, the percentages of people who had negative comments about hotel fell. The most dramatic fall was in the answer satisfactory by 28% by 28% was in the answer for satisfactory. There was a decline in the figure for the opinion that poor for poor satisfaction. In addition, the Parkway Hotel saw a dramatic decrease in the rates of visitors felt who felt the service was very poor, which was the lowest – 4% in 2010.

SAMPLE 15

The first chart below shows how energy is used in an average Australian household. The second chart shows the greenhouse gas emissions which result from this energy use.

Summarise the information by selecting and reporting the main features, and make comparisons where relevant.

Source: http://www.ielts-mentor.com/writing-sample/academic-writing-task-1/2418-energy-use-in-an-average-australian-household

The percentage of household energy use in Australia:

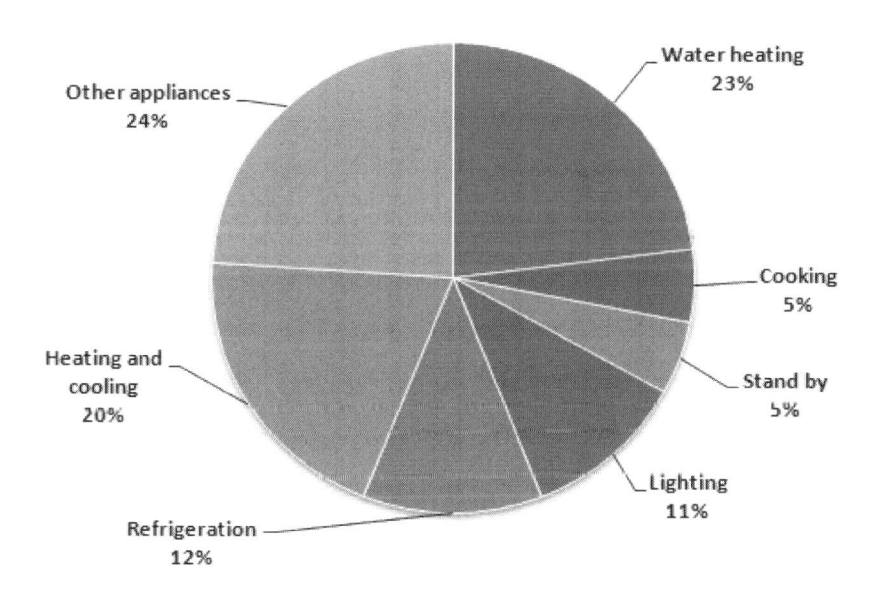

- Water heating 23%
- Cooking 5%
- Stand by 5%
- Lighting 11%
- Refrigeration 12%
- Heating and cooling 20%
- Other appliances 24%

The percentage of greenhouse gas produced in Australia:

Other appliances
16%

Water heating
25%

Cooking
4%

Stand by
3%

Lighting
7%

Refrigeration
7%

Heating and cooling
38%

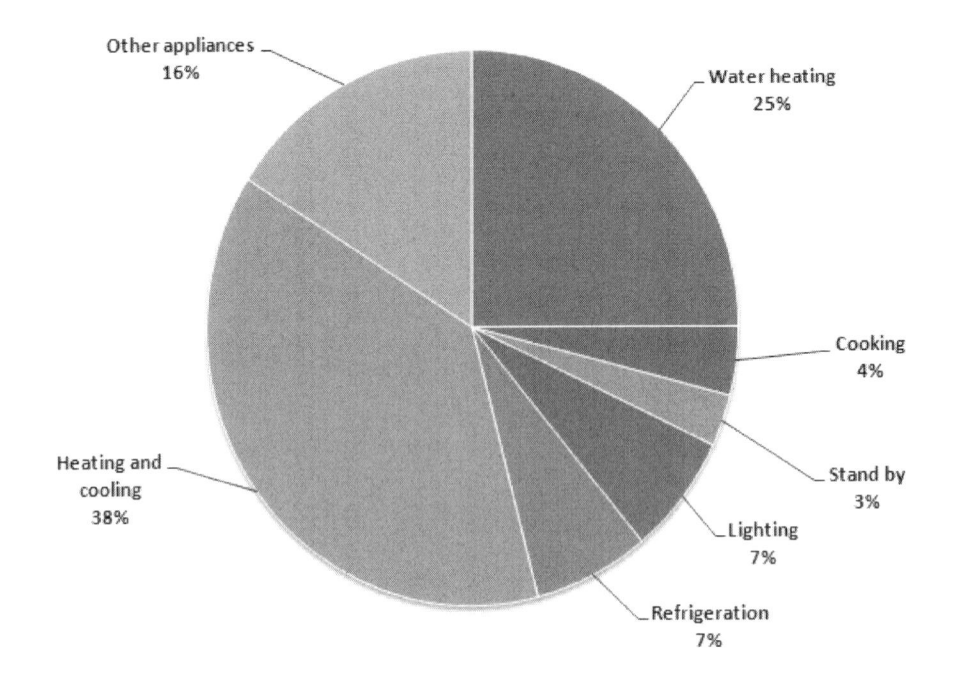

Original essay:

The first chart below indicates energy consumptions in an average Australian household while the other illustrates how much greenhouse gas emissions produced from those uses.

Overall, the figures in using energy and emitting greenhouse gas are quite different with those types such as heating, other appliances, lighting and refrigeration. While there are small changes in the figures for others.

Fistly, The using energy for heating and other appliances are about 42% and 15% but the emissions emit from those activitites change a lot with only 15% for heating and 28% from the other appliances, the highest recorded in emitting greenhouse gas proportion.

Secondly, Those activites comsumming energy such as lighting and refrigeration seems like produce more greenhouse effects than the energy they use. Lighting, for instance, emit as twice as the energy they use (4%

and 8%).While refrigeration only comsume 7% but emit 14% gas emissions.

The last two figures are water heating which is the second large source of comsumming energy and cooling, the smallest figure in using energy. There are no big changes between energy used and gas.

Edited essay:

The first chart below indicates ~~the~~ energy consumption~~s~~ in an average Australian household while the ~~other~~ second illustrates how much greenhouse gas ~~emissions produced~~ is emitted from those uses.

Overall, the figures ~~in~~ for using energy and emitting greenhouse gas are quite different with those types ~~such as~~ namely heating, other appliances, lighting and refrigeration. ~~While~~ Meanwhile, there are small changes in the figures for others.

~~Fistly, The using energy~~ The amount of energy used for heating and other appliances are about 42% and 15% but ~~the emissions emit~~ the figures for emissions from those activities change a lot with only 15% for heating and 28% from the other appliances ,which is the highest recorded in emitting greenhouse gas proportion.

~~Secondly,~~Those activities consuming energy such as lighting and refrigeration seems ~~like~~ to produce more greenhouse effects than the energy they use. Lighting, for instance, emits as twice as the energy they use (4% and 8%).~~While~~ Meanwhile, refrigeration only comsume 7% but emit 14% gas emissions.

The last two figures are water heating which is the second large source of ~~comsumming energy~~ energy consumption and cooling, which is the smallest figure in using energy. There are no ~~big~~ large changes between energy used and gas emitted.

45

SAMPLE 16

The charts below show the number of girls per 100 boys in all levels of education.

Summarize the information by selecting and reporting on the main features, and make comparisons where relevant.

Source: http://www.ielts-exam.net/academic_writing_samples_task_1/671/

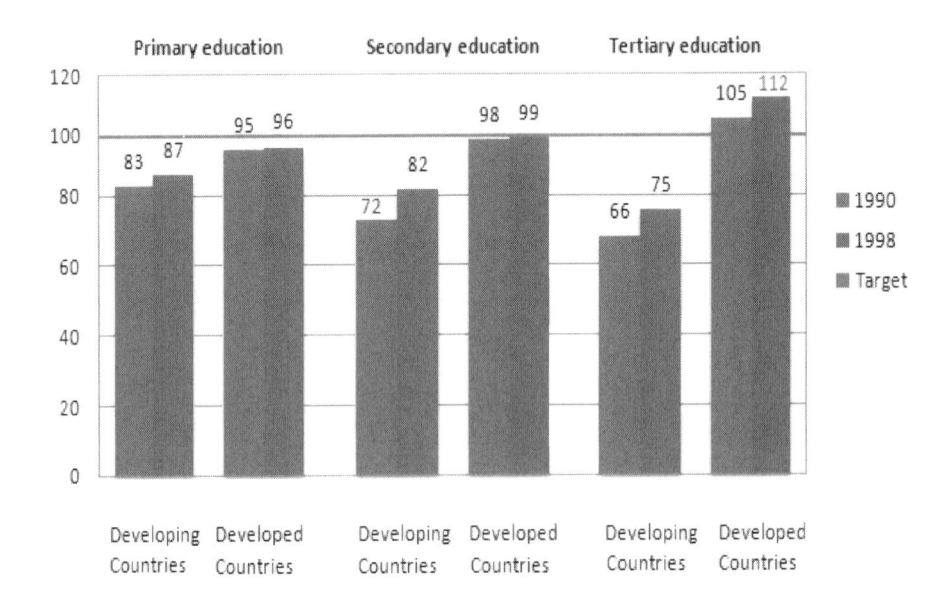

Original essay:

The charts illustrates the number of girls per 100 boys in primary, secondary and tertiary education. In general, there were more girls than boys studying in all levels of education and, their appearance tended to increase from 1990 to 2000 in both developing and developed countries.

Obviously, in the period of 1990 to 2000, the developing countries experienced significant increase in secondary and tertiary level respectively;

from 72 in 1990 to 82 in 2000 and from 66 in 1990 to 75 in 2000. Meanwhile, it was witnessed in developed countries the sharp rise in the first two levels of education: from 93 in 1990 to 96 in 2000 in primary education and from 98 in 1990 to 99 in 2000 in secondary level.

On the other hand, it was highlighted in the tertiary school enrolment chart that there was even a worse balance in developed countries since the number of girls were 105 in 1990 and subsequently rose to 116 in 2000 per 100 boys at that time.

Edited essay:

The charts illustrates the number of girls per 100 boys in primary, secondary and tertiary education. In general, there were more girls than boys studying in all levels of education and, their ~~appearance~~ participation tended to increase from 1990 to 2000 in both developing and developed countries.

Obviously, in the period of 1990 to 2000, the developing countries experienced a significant increase in the number of girls (for example) secondary and tertiary level respectively; from 72 in 1990 to 82 in 2000 and from 66 in 1990 to 75 in 2000. Meanwhile, ~~it was witnessed in developed countries the~~ developed countries witnessed a sharp rise in the first two levels of education: from 93 in 1990 to 96 in 2000 in primary education and from 98 in 1990 to 99 in 2000 in secondary level.

On the other hand, it was highlighted in the tertiary school enrolment chart that there was ~~even a wor~~se balance an imbalance in developed countries since the number of girls were 105 in 1990 and subsequently rose to ~~116 in 2000 per 100 boys~~ 116 per 100 boys in 2000 at that time.

SAMPLE 17

The chart below shows the amount of money per week spent on fast foods in Britain. The graph shows the trends in consumption of fast foods.

Source: http://www.ielts-exam.net/academic_writing_samples_task_1/129/

Expenditure on Fast Foods by Income Groups, UK 1990

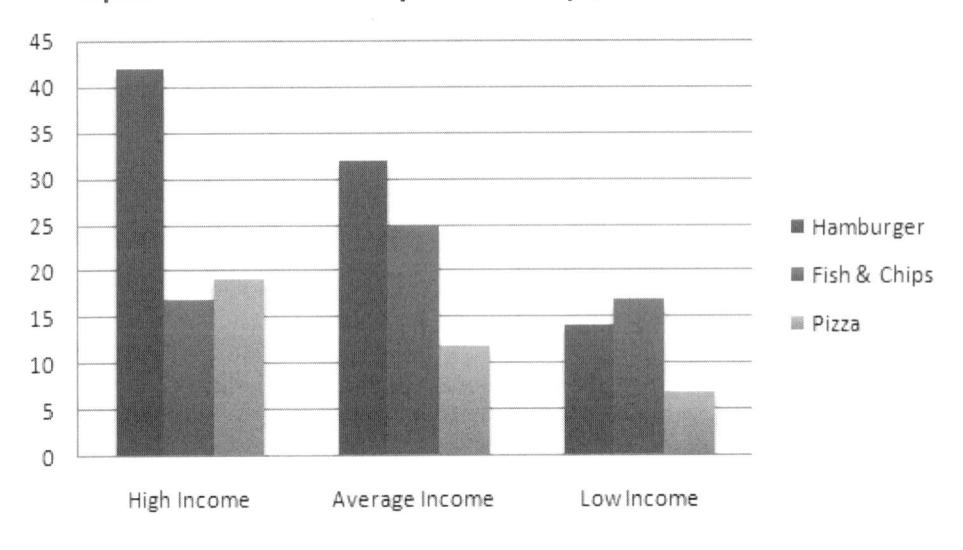

Income Group	Hamburger	Fish & Chips	Pizza
High Income	42	17	19
Average Income	32	25	12
Low Income	14	17	7

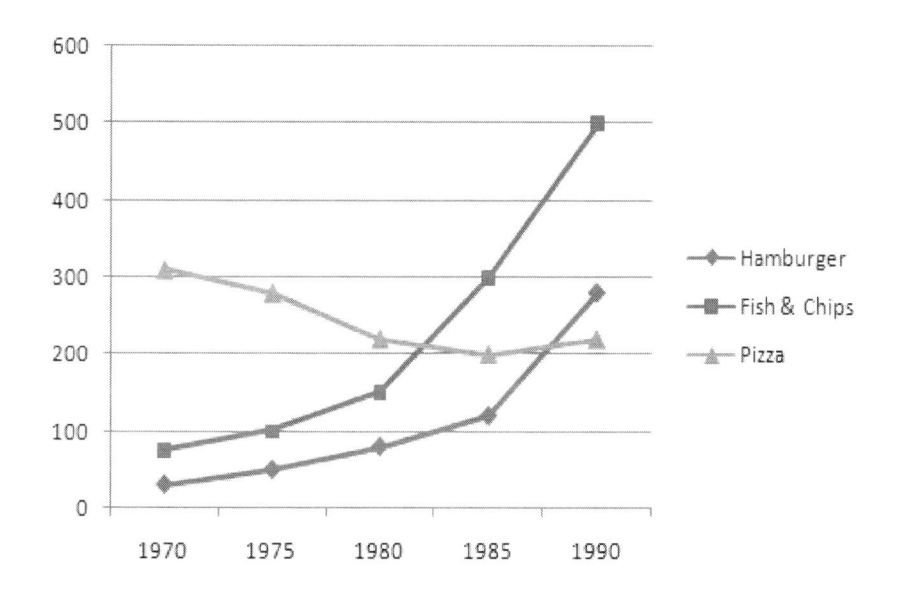

Original essay:

The table gives information about money per week which British spending on hamburger, fish & chips, and pizza in 1990 while the line graph compares changes in consumption of these items during the period of 20 years.

Overall, the amount of money spent on hamburger in a high income group was the highest, and fish & chips was the most consumed item in 1990.

In 1990, high income group people spending money on humberger is nearly 42 pence per person, above 2 times higher than the figures for fish & chips and pizza, at roughly 17 and 19 pence respectively. By contrast, about 17 pence of low income U.K. population paid for fish & chips in comparision with around 14 pence of humberger and approximately 7 pence of pizza. Humberger was also the most popular fast food in the medium income class people, they spent over 32 pence on this item while they only spent 25 pence on fish & chips and above 10 pence on pizza.

Over the 20-year period, fish & chips consumption experienced a dramatic increase from roughly 75 gm to 500 gm, and the consumption of humburger also rose rapidly by approximately 250 gm. In contrast, pizza was the highest consumed fast food in 1970 with above 300 gm, and then declined to about 200 gm in 1990.

Edited essay:

The table gives information about money per week which British ~~spending~~ spent on hamburger, fish & chips, and pizza in 1990 while the line graph compares changes in consumption of these items during the period of 20 years.

Overall, the amount of money spent on hamburger in a high income group was the highest, and fish & chips was the most consumed item in 1990.

In 1990, ~~high income group people spending money on~~ the money people with high income used for buying ~~humberger~~ hamburger ~~is~~ was nearly 42 pence per person, above 2 times higher than the figures for fish & chips and pizza, at roughly 17 and 19 pence respectively. By contrast, about 17 pence of low income U.K. population paid for fish & chips in ~~comparision~~ comparison with around 14 pence of ~~humberger~~ hamburger and approximately 7 pence of pizza. ~~Humberger~~ Hamburger was also the most popular fast food in the medium income class ~~people~~, they spent over 32 pence on this item while they only spent 25 pence on fish & chips and above 10 pence on pizza.

Over the 20-year period, fish & chips consumption experienced a dramatic increase from roughly 75 gm to 500 gm, and the consumption of ~~humburger~~ hamburger also rose rapidly by approximately 250 gm. In contrast, pizza was the highest consumed fast food in 1970 with above 300 gm, and then declined to about 200 gm in 1990.

SAMPLE 18

The chart below shows the total number of minutes (in millions) of telephone calls in Finland, divided into three categories, from 1995 – 2004.

Summarise the information by selecting and reporting the main features, and make comparisons where relevant.

Source: http://www.ielts-exam.net/academic_writing_samples_task_1/716/

Finland's telephone calls, by category, 1995 - 2004

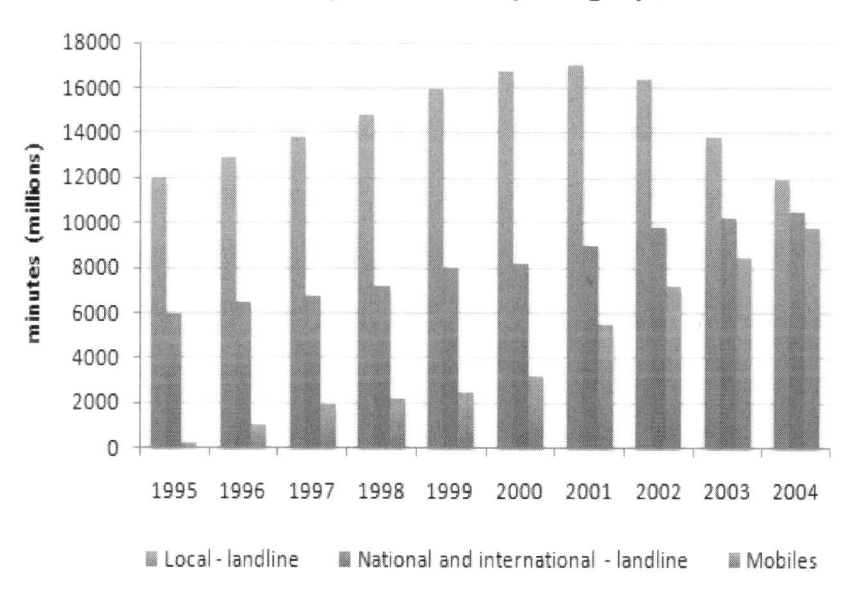

[Bar chart showing minutes (millions) on y-axis from 0 to 18000, years 1995-2004 on x-axis, with three categories: Local - landline, National and international - landline, Mobiles]

Original essay:

The chart illustrates the amount of time (in million minutes) people spending on 3 different types of telephone calls in Filand between 1995 and 2004.

Overall, using local landline always dominated among 3 categories in the shown period. However the difference among groups became less at the end of the given time.

In 1995, the number for local landline group was exact 12000 which doulbed that of national and international landline. Then these 2 groups saw the similar pattern of constant growth to peak at 17000 in local landline group and reach about 9000 in national and international landline in 2001. After that, while local landline started to decrease to12000 the same point of the beginning of the period, national and international landline group continued to increase to nearly 10500.

Mobiles started the period at very low number of about 200, which was far less than remnant groups but saw constant dramatic growth over the given period to reach nearly 9800 in 2004, reducing the gaps with the others to a much smaller numbers than the beginning.

Edited essay:

The ~~chart~~ diagram illustrates the amount of time (in million minutes) people ~~spending~~ spent on 3 different types of telephone calls in Finland between 1995 and 2004.

Overall, ~~using~~ local landline always dominated ~~among 3 categories~~ telephone usage in the shown period. However the ~~difference~~ gap among groups ~~became less~~ was narrowed down at the end of the given time.

In 1995, the ~~number~~ figure for local landline group was exactly 12000 which doubled that of national and international landline. Then these 2 groups saw the similar pattern of constant growth to peak at 17000 ~~in local landline group~~ for the former and reach about 9000 in ~~national and international landline~~ the latter in 2001. After that, while local landline started to decrease to 12000, the same level as the beginning of the period ~~same point of the beginning of the period~~, national and international landline group continued to increase to nearly 10500.

Mobiles started the period at very low number of about 200, which was far less than ~~remnant~~ the other two groups but ~~saw constant dramatic growth~~ experienced the most dramatic rise over the given period to reach nearly 9800 in 2004, ~~reducing the gaps with the others to a much smaller numbers than the beginning~~ making themselves as popular a choice of communication as local, national and international landlines.

SAMPLE 19

The graph and table below show the average monthly temperatures and the average number of hours of sunshine per year in three major cities.

Summarize the information by selecting and reporting the main features and make comparisons where relevant.

Source: http://www.ielts-mentor.com/writing-sample/academic-writing-task-1/1805-academic-ielts-writing-task-1-sample-142-average-monthly-temperatures-and-the-average-number-of-hours-of-sunshine

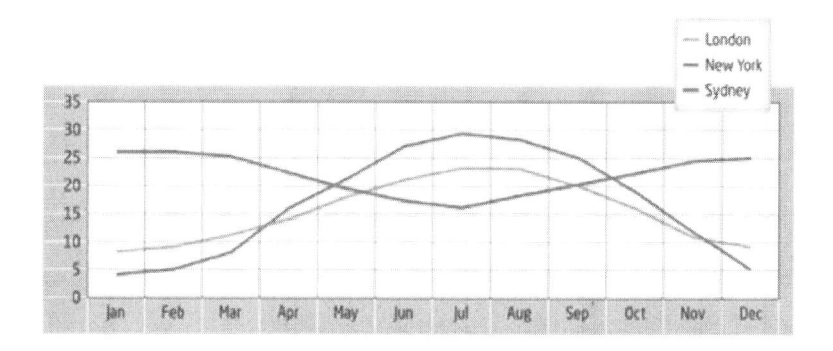

Total annual hours of sunshine for London, New York and Sydney

London	1,180
New York	2,535
Sydney	2,473

Original essay:

A glance at the charts reveals the average temperature on a monthly basis together with the annual daylight on average in London, New York and Sydney.

Overall, while New York and London witness quite a similar pattern, temperature of Sydney fluctuate in a different trend ; however, the number of daylight hours in all metropolises is proportional to temperatures, by extension, they have experienced a similar level at the very beginning and the very end, whereas they have changed significantly in the mid of the year.

In details, the longest time of daylight has gone on New York, but the temperature in this place starts the year at the lowest level, with roughly 5 degrees before going up gradually until peaking at approximately 30 degrees in July, then falling back to the starting point at the end of the year. Despite having the shortest day, London has the temperature almost doubling the figure for the former at the beginning, following with the same attitude towards temperatures' trend in New York.

As the city with the second most hours of sunshine, expectedly, Sydney is supposed to be the hottest place, namely more or less 25 degrees during three first months. There is a gradual decline in temperatures of Sydney, however, at the mid of the year before reaching a bottom at about 15 degrees. After that, the temperature in this city has risen gradually then recovered thoroughly to finish the year.

Edited essay:

A glance at the charts reveals the average temperature on a monthly basis together with ~~the annual daylight on average~~ (or: the annual average daylight) in London, New York and Sydney.

Overall, while New York and London witness quite a similar pattern, temperature of Sydney ~~fluctuate in a different trend~~ had an opposite trend; however, the number of daylight hours in all metropolises is proportional to temperatures, by extension, they have experienced a similar level at the very beginning and the very end, whereas they have changed significantly in the mid of the year.

Suggested Overview: Overall, while New York and London witness the same trend, the fluctuations in the temperature of New York are more significant. Moreover, New York is also the cities with the longest hours of sunshine.

In details, the longest time of daylight ~~has gone on~~ belong to New York,

~~but~~ the temperature in this place starts ~~the year~~ at the lowest level, with roughly 5 degrees before going up gradually until peaking at approximately 30 degrees in July, then falling back to the starting point at the end of the year. Despite having the shortest day, London has the temperature almost doubling the figure for the former at the beginning, following with the same ~~attitude~~ trend towards temperatures' trend in New York.

As the city with the second most hours of sunshine, expectedly, Sydney is supposed to be the hottest place, namely more or less 25 degrees during three first months. There is a gradual decline in temperatures of Sydney, however, at the mid of the year before reaching a bottom at about 15 degrees. After that, the temperature in this city has risen gradually then recovered thoroughly to finish the year.

Suggested: At the same time, there are 2473 hours of sunshine in Sydney. Therefore, its temperature remains fairly constant at around 20 degrees. Specifically, starting at 25 degree, the temperature drop to the lowest point of 15 degrees in July before recovering in the last year.

Sample essay:

http://www.ielts-mentor.com/writing-sample/academic-writing-task-1/1805-academic-ielts-writing-task-1-sample-142-average-monthly-temperatures-and-the-average-number-of-hours-of-sunshine

SAMPLE 20

The line graph below shows the average daily maximum temperatures for Auckland and Christchurch, two cities in New Zealand, and London and Edinburgh, two cities in the United Kingdom.

Summarise the information by selecting and reporting the main features, and make comparisons where relevant.

Source: http://www.testbig.com/ielts-writing-task-i-essays/line-graph-below-shows-average-daily-maximum-temperatures-auckland-and

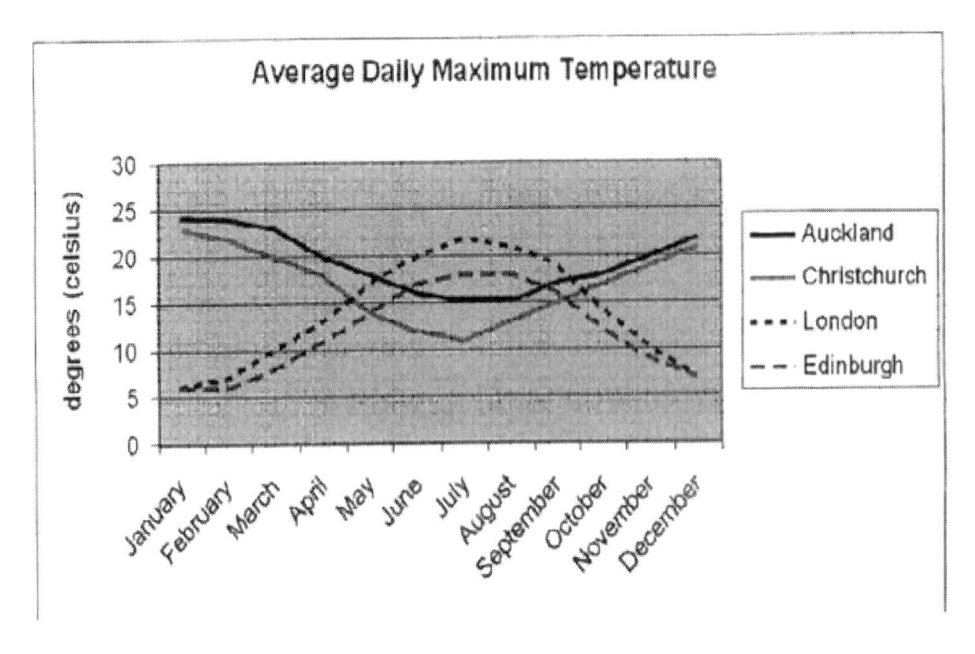

Average Daily Maximum Temperature

Original essay:

The line charts illustrate some information about the daily hottest degree in four cities. As can be seen from the run chart that, the trend of temperature is similar in one country's cities.

To turn to New Zealand, the temperature in Auckland is higher than Christchurch. Between January and July, there is a downward trend of about 10 celsius in the temperature of Auckland. Similarly, Christchurch's temperature sinks to a low of roughly 15 celsius. Afterward, the degree in Auckland remains stable at approximately 15 celsius before increasing significantly to well over 20 celsius while that in Christchurch rockets to more or less 20 celsius.

In London, from over 5 celsius, the temperature rises sharply and reaches a peak of roughly 23 celsius before falls gradually to nearly 10 celsius. The degree increases slightly to over 15 celsius and remains constant at this level before plunging to about 8 celsius in Edinburgh.

Edited essay:

The line chart~~s~~ illustrates some information about the daily hottest degree in four cities. As can be seen from ~~the run chart~~ the graph that, ~~the trend of temperature is similar in one country's cities~~ while the two cities in New Zealand (Auckland and Christchurch) have the same pattern, the remaining in UK witness a completely opposite trend.

To turn to/Concerning New Zealand, the temperature in Auckland is higher than Christchurch throughout the year at 25 and 23 respectively. Between January and July, there is a downward trend of about 10 Celsius in the temperature of Auckland. Similarly, Christchurch's temperature sinks to a low of roughly 15 Celsius. Afterward, the degree in Auckland remains stable at approximately 15 Celsius before increasing significantly to well over 20 Celsius while that in Christchurch also rockets to more or less/around 20 Celsius.

In London, from over 5 Celsius, the temperature rises sharply and reaches a peak of roughly 23 Celsius before falls falling gradually to nearly ~~10~~ 5 Celsius. The degree increases slightly to over 15 Celsius and remains constant at this level before plunging to about 8 Celsius in Edinburgh.

CONCLUSION

Thank you again for downloading this book on *"Ielts Writing Task 1 Corrections: Most Common Mistakes Students Make And How To Avoid Them (Book 1)"* and reading all the way to the end. I'm extremely grateful.

If you know of anyone else who may benefit from the informative tips presented in this book, please help me inform them of this book. I would greatly appreciate it.

Finally, if you enjoyed this book and feel that it has added value to your study in any way, please take a couple of minutes to share your thoughts and post a REVIEW on Amazon. Your feedback will help me to continue to write the kind of Kindle books that helps you get results. Furthermore, if you write a simple REVIEW with positive words for this book on Amazon, you can help hundreds or perhaps thousands of other readers who may want to enhance their study results have a chance getting what they need. Like you, they worked hard for every penny they spend on books. With the information and recommendation you provide, they would be more likely to take action right away. We really look forward to reading your review.

Thanks again for your support and good luck!

If you enjoy my book, please write a POSITIVE REVIEW on amazon.

-- Johnny Chuong –

CHECK OUT OTHER BOOKS

Go here to check out other related books that might interest you:

https://www.amazon.com/dp/B06W2P6S22

Marriage Heat: 7 Secrets Every Married Couple Should Know On How To Fix Intimacy Problems, Spice Up Marriage & Be Happy Forever

https://www.amazon.com/dp/B01ITSW8YU

Smart Kids Smart Money: The Ultimate Parent's Guide To Teaching Kids About Earning, Saving, Giving, Spending And Investing Money Wisely

https://www.amazon.com/dp/B01KEZVFU4

Legal Vocabulary In Use: Master 600+ Essential Legal Terms And Phrases Explained In 10 Minutes A Day

http://www.amazon.com/dp/B01L0FKXPU

Shortcut To Ielts Writing: The Ultimate Guide To Immediately Increase Your Ielts Writing Scores

http://www.amazon.com/dp/B01JV7EQGG

Legal Terminology And Phrases: Essential Legal Terms Explained You Need To Know About Crimes, Penalty And Criminal Procedure

http://www.amazon.com/dp/B01L5EB54Y

Productivity Secrets For Students: The Ultimate Guide To Improve Your Mental Concentration, Kill Procrastination, Boost Memory And Maximize Productivity In Study

http://www.amazon.com/dp/B01JS52UT6

Daughter of Strife: 7 Techniques On How To Win Back Your Stubborn Teenage Daughter

https://www.amazon.com/dp/B01HS5E3V6

Parenting Teens With Love And Logic: A Survival Guide To Overcoming The Barriers Of Adolescence About Dating, Sex And Substance Abuse

https://www.amazon.com/dp/B01JQUTNPM

Female Organism: The Best Oral Sex Ever To Give Her A Mind-Blowing Pleasure

https://www.amazon.com/dp/B01KIOVC18

http://www.amazon.com/dp/B01J7G5IVS

http://www.amazon.com/dp/B01K0ARNA4

Printed in Great Britain
by Amazon